W9-BBO-568

The Spirit of May

Books by
J.-J. Servan-Schreiber

LIEUTENANT IN ALGERIA

THE AMERICAN CHALLENGE

THE SPIRIT OF MAY

J.-J. Servan-Schreiber

THE SPIRIT
OF MAY

Translated from the French by Ronald Steel

McGraw-Hill Book Company

New York   St. Louis   San Francisco
Toronto   Mexico City   Panama

Preface

If the explosion that rocked France in May 1968 had been merely something peculiar and totally unpredictable, like a bolt of lightning in a clear sky, it would have meant little and soon have been forgotten.

But even though no one could have predicted when it would strike and the form it would take, the reasons for this upheaval are anchored deep in French society. A good many people, among them sociologists, economists, professors, and scientists, warned us long ago that it was likely to happen.

In hopes of throwing some light on this upheaval, and to avoid any mistaken idea that it was somehow "accidental," I have included a few extracts from *The American Challenge*, which was published a few months earlier. These extracts, included in the Appendix to this book, simply restate the opinion of French experts and show that the disease was critical, that it had indeed been diagnosed, and that it was rooted in contemporary conditions and one day had to split wide open.

We shall soon face the task of building a different society in a different Europe. A great many men whose names are still unfamiliar will take part in this great effort and, wherever they are, will direct it. Before the architects of the new society begin their political reckoning, I would like to reflect on the crisis. These comments were written and published during those

traumatic days between the thirteenth of May
and the second of June.

We are racing against the clock. We must
move fast to establish the links between the underlying problems and the explosion that took
place, between the France we know and the revolt that seized the nation by surprise, between
the magnificent dreams of our young people and
the constraining imperatives of economic development. We must, in short, make all Europeans
aware of what is happening—Europeans who
once again are being summoned to join the front
ranks of history, even though they are still satisfied nonchalantly to bring up the rear.

J.-J. Servan-Schreiber

Contents

Preface   vii

1. From Dialogue to Power   1
2. Challenge and Rebirth   11
3. The Second Industrial Revolution   19
4. The Explosion of May   27
5. Between Withdrawal and Movement   35
6. Development and Democracy   45
7. Business and the University   53
8. The Act of Confidence   61
9. Without Hate or Fear   67
10. From Spain to Sweden   77

APPENDIX
1. The Essence of the *Challenge*   87
2. Answers to *Life*   99

1

From Dialogue to Power

Nothing is so intimidating as outraged youth. When the young shout and rebel against society, few people dare take them on—which is as it should be.

From the plethora of analyses of the student rebellion, we can sort out a few important conclusions.

1. When tens of thousands of students join together in protest even though they face a great risk of violent reprisals, their actions cannot be

dismissed by any pat explanation—whether it be denouncing "agitators" and "extremists" or criticizing the lack of "reforms" in the universities. Such a powerful rebellion demands an explanation that goes to the source.

2. Responsibility, if we may say so, lies with those who are in responsible positions—those who have had the power to do or not to do things since the liberation of France twenty-three years ago. The problem will not be solved by changing the dean of a graduate faculty or by persuading the Minister of Education to practice self-criticism. Our society is a mess, and can be rebuilt only by starting from the bottom and working up. This is, above all, a political problem.

3. Our very conception of tradition and authority has been inevitably dislocated by the rapid scientific and technological transformation of contemporary life, by the mounting pace of change in everything from mathematics to industry. Education can no longer be authoritar-

ian, either in the family or in the school. It must be based on new forms of *dialogue*.

These observations are no longer news to anyone, but it is not a bad idea to keep repeating them. Eventually we may begin to pay attention. Perhaps the best way of clarifying the problem would be to pause for a moment on the key word *dialogue*. It was a beautiful word—one whose meaning now seems to have been lost.

When the government sends the police into the Sorbonne to "establish a dialogue"; when thousands of students attack public institutions, led by many who sneer at dialogue as simply a trick; when "We want a dialogue" becomes the battle cry of conservatives and "No dialogue for us" the chant of rebels; when the very idea of a dialogue becomes a dividing line between those who are content with the present order and those who want to overturn it—then the problem goes a long way beyond semantics.

Dialogue is indispensable. But it must rest upon confidence. It cannot take place unless each participant is convinced that the other will carry out the decisions reached. Otherwise it is simply letting off steam.

Yet confidence is what is in doubt. Dialogue becomes impossible. At least until it can be based on something that will re-create lost confidence—until people can be assured of participating in decision-making and controlling the way decisions are enacted.

Everything else stems from the loss of confidence, and it is not hard to trace it to its source. For as long as any adult today can remember, or even his father can recall, politics has often been little more than lies. Not only in France, but everywhere in Europe.

For the past seventy-five years French politicians have been lying about the Colonial Empire, which was both an instrument of oppression and a drain on the country's wealth. They lied about the Glorious Victory of 1918, which was paid for by a carnage so terrible that the nation has been suffering from it ever since. They lied about the "good management" of Poincaré's successors who, under the pretext of price stability, succeeded in debilitating France by reducing her industrial production by 20 per cent between the two wars—incredible as it now seems. They lied at the time of the famous Popular Front, just before World War II, which started out by abandoning the Spanish Republicans and ended by leading France to Munich and the collaboration of Marshal Pétain with Hitler. They lied during the Liberation when, instead of allowing an aroused and clear-headed popular will to assert itself in a nation finally awakened by the mistakes and misadventures of the past, they infected us with the bleeding ulcer of colonial wars in Vietnam and Algeria and the leukemia of inflation. They lied on the sixth of February 1956, when Prime Minister Guy Mollet went to Algiers and capitulated before the violence of the French settlers. They lied again on the thirteenth of May 1958 when the French army in Algeria launched a *coup d'état* against the government in Paris and called on General de Gaulle to assume power. And they are still lying today, on both sides of the political fence, when the Right trumpets its demands for political independence from America, at the same time it abandons to foreign corporations the economic foundations of independence—or when the Left still looks wistfully toward Soviet bureaucracy as though it offered a path to justice and plenty.

After decades of lies it is almost impossible to have a dialogue based on confidence. The farmers no longer have any, the miners and post office employees don't have any, and the students have even less.

The same is true for political groups in Germany, which have been shaken by even more terrible experiences and which today often engage in even more blatant political deals. It is true for Italian universities, where the teaching staff is distinguished by its indifference to financial honesty. And of course it is true for Spain and Poland, where the official lie is not merely a technique used by those who hold power—it is what power is all about.

The question, then, all over Europe, is no longer about the content of "reforms." This, like the "internal autonomy" France once bestowed so grandly upon her former colonies, is not even worth sneering at. Nor is it even a matter of working out reforms through free discussion, for the necessary credit was used up long ago. The problem is power itself.

Power now must be broken up and redistributed. This is the only way we can hold our society together. Otherwise there will be dislocation and a retrogression that could swallow up an entire generation in a terrible waste of energy and

intelligence, just as Stalinism bled three genera-
tions of Russians.

The only way we can hope to avoid social dis-
orientation is by diffusing political responsibility. This means distributing it in new ways. We
are now truly in a prerevolutionary situation.

2
Challenge and Rebirth

It takes someone completely satisfied with society as it is—indeed, an incorrigible optimist supremely confident of everlasting progress —to agree with Raymond Aron's judgment of the May revolt. "From a historical point of view," he has written, "the present upheaval involves more risks than hopes."

What the student revolt disturbed, and perhaps smashed, was not the smooth unrolling of the second industrial revolution in France and throughout Europe, but rather a deadly process of slow decay and mindless abdication.

Looking at the insurrection from a corporate perspective—the reform of the universities—we can see aspects full of danger and demagoguery; but from a political perspective this challenge to traditional industrial society "involves more risks than hopes."

This situation can perhaps be put in its true perspective by comparing it to the turbulence in the fifteenth century that culminated in the first Renaissance. The distinguishing feature of society 500 years ago, just as today, was the introduction of new technology. This caused such changes in people's lives and their environment that they needed a new definition of society. The invention of the printing press, the most important development of the age, overturned all the traditional ways of exchanging information, revolutionized the idea man had of his relationship with others and finally his concept of self.

CHALLENGE AND REBIRTH

In our age the invention of computer-linked information systems is, in most areas of industry and research, changing our methods for transmitting ideas, bringing together for the first time the various factors that go into decision-making, and redistributing intellectual power. This is leading to a radical critique of traditional industrial society.

In every major period of history there has been a close link between changes in the way we do things and the way we approach life. Professor André Latreille has recently described the basic characteristics of the Renaissance: "Not only were the fifteenth and sixteenth centuries the age of artists and writers, but also the age of invention—from the engineers who perfected instruments of war or developed new kinds of ships to the planners who worked out ambitious models for urban development or envisaged methods of business management. It is surprising to see the number of technical books in which innovation was preached. This phenomenon, which could be called the genesis of capitalism, is of great social importance."

This could just as easily be an analysis of what has happened within the last few years in our modern industrial world: the incessant transformation of methods, and then of ideas themselves, by scientific and technological innovation, above all by the remarkable triumph of electronic information systems which have globalized science, research, and knowledge with incalculable intellectual consequences.

This second Renaissance, coming 500 years after the first, has bypassed an indifferent Europe. Not only has the baton of power been passed on to the Russians and the Americans, but gradually so have the science of invention itself and the art of organizing talent, the model on which our modern civilization is being molded. This abdication, which spreads from technology to philosophy, is the stigma of Europe in our age. It is what we must combat before any more time is lost.

Months before the riots at Nanterre and the Sorbonne, the universities at Milan and Barcelona, at Turin, Madrid, and Berlin were shaken by similar disturbances. The reasons are the same all over. A powerful historical tide overrides local troubles, reforms, and parochial political problems.

For more than a generation Europe, and France in the heart of Europe, has been a passive observer of history rather than a participant. For a continent so rich in men and resources, this situation is becoming increasingly intolerable. With a leadership class intellectually obsessed with an American pattern it copies clumsily with a fifteen-year lag, and with a working class equally obsessed by a Soviet pattern whose disastrous rigidity has been obvious in Eastern Europe for several years, the nations of Western Europe have looked like—and still look like—psychologically conquered territories.

This state of intellectual resignation, this technological inferiority that is really a cultural surrender, has left us standing by the wayside as others have taken on the tasks of our age. It has made us incapable of building an original model of industrial society that would be more humane than the models that are being offered us and eventually will be imposed upon us.

3
The Second Industrial Revolution

For the past few years the most important issue has been the confrontation of a particularly rigid social and political order with an accelerating technological, scientific—and therefore intellectual—transformation.

The first industrial revolution in France occurred in a country which, fifteen years ago, was still largely rural. The second industrial revolution—atomic energy, automation, space communications, computers—is now bypassing the very areas that have been most advanced. The breaking down of frontiers in the Common Market has forced the industries of France and Europe to adapt or perish.

At the same time, the population explosion, even more powerful in France than in her neighbors, has shaken the structure of society—particularly the universities and the major cities, which were planned for far fewer people.

Add to this a psychological mutation. None of the eighteenth- or nineteenth-century ideologies are able to cope with the new problems of society. Pure capitalism is no longer satisfactory, and it is changing rapidly in the United States. Socialism, as it has been practiced in Eastern Europe, has also failed and is going through a radical transformation in Russia itself. The problem facing the French is confronting all Europeans.

Until the explosion of May 1968, French society was strikingly resistant to change. This rigidity took (and still takes) two forms.

There was, first, a kind of mutual-assurance society against change. This was sought by leadership groups which formed a conspiracy to restrict membership in the oligarchy to which they belonged and also to limit risks by collective action. Nearly all professions and business firms have engaged in such restrictive practices.

Second, society has been structured on distant centers of authority whose decisions are not subject to question. The authoritarianism of the bosses and the irresponsibility of their subordinates form a mutually reinforcing pair. This is true to such a degree that last year I could write in *The American Challenge:* "The presumption of incompetence produces its own confirmation, for it does not allow those it affects the opportunity to demonstrate or acquire the expertise which they are refused *a priori.* It breeds irresponsible conduct, thus justifying the suspicion on which it is based."

People live in isolation at each level of the hierarchy, with each group enjoying its own special privileges, whether they be great or small, and each separated as much as possible from the rest, the ensemble being a juxtaposition of castes and clans. Since centralization is the norm, any change in the system is virtually impossible.

Those who live in the provinces resent this humiliating and paralyzing centralization even more than Parisians do. In nearly all neighboring countries, such as Italy, Germany, and Britain, a great many problems are resolved at the local level. In France, however, no mayor or municipal council would dare make a decision without the support of Paris or the approval of the regional guardians appointed by the central government. Whether the subject be education, housing, urban planning, the water supply, or recreational equipment, the municipalities have had virtually no freedom. Elected officials are condemned to play the role of intermediaries between the local population and the impersonal government bureaus whose favors they beseech. Initiative is stifled, responsibility is diluted, and the dissatisfied citizens have no recourse other than to blame authorities who are impossible to identify. *They* are the ones to blame; *they* refuse to give us the funds we need. Citizens have the right to accuse, to complain, and to threaten, but they have no authority to change the system under which they live.

Caught in this crossfire between a mounting pace of change and a petrified society, the nation has tried to follow two contradictory objectives at the same time: the expansion of the economy and the conservation of the old political mechanism.

This mechanism was not destroyed sooner because it protected traditional ways of doing things to which the French have been, and still are, deeply attached. There is a kind of individualism that is more at ease in irresponsible argument or in the arms of absolute authority than in continual negotiation, compromise, and team-work.

Yet the idea of growth, well-being, and steady progress—the hallmark of our age throughout the entire industrial world, both in the East and in the West—has now been so embedded in our minds that no one is seriously willing to consider calling a halt to economic expansion. So where do we go?

4

The Explosion of May

The movement of students and workers that erupted in Paris in May 1968 was not a movement primarily designed to win material benefits. Naturally there were underlying demands involving the standard of living which found an opportunity to come to the surface during the fervor of insurrection. But these demands explain neither the outbreak of the phenomenon nor the way it spread so quickly and naturally from the students to the workers.

This was not a "socialist" movement, as the term is applied traditionally and so dogmatically in Eastern Europe. It did not demand the installation of a "people's democracy." What it dared to question was not the legitimacy of property, which was treated as a secondary problem, but, above all, power and authority. It made no attempt to seize the means of production, but rather the centers of command. Everything took place as if those who joined the insurrection understood that the crucial issue in today's battle is not property but power.

This movement above all involved a fundamental questioning of the present forms of authority—of all authority. Here we can see a classic manifestation of the French demon of anarchy, which is only the other side of authoritarianism, both its cause and its effect. We can also see the contrary, a demand for dignity which leads naturally to a quest for responsibility.

THE EXPLOSION OF MAY

All Frenchmen who do not have the luck to belong to one of the ruling oligarchies suffer from being treated as minors. "The dispute is not simply over personalities or institutions," Pierre Mendès-France said in May. "It also dramatizes the determination of millions of Frenchmen no longer to be considered impotent subjects in a harsh, inhumane, conservative society, but rather to perform their own role freely in a society they can look upon as really their own."

Authority feels obliged to lie to those it considers overgrown children. When technological change threatens some area of industry or agriculture, the government does not dare tell the truth to employers, and they in turn dare not tell the truth to their workers. Instead of putting their cards on the table and systematically preparing for conversion, using all the resources necessary for the job and joining with all those whose jobs and standards of living are at stake, they instead try to make do with decrepit structures in the most second-rate, wretched fashion until the whole thing collapses, bringing unemployment and financial disaster. Everyone loses all around. Yet a little bit of foresight and confidence in the good sense of those directly involved would have made it possible to work out solutions more humane and also more practical.

The demand for self-determination is widespread. It is a reaction against the straitjacket of impersonal regulations whose origins and purpose are a mystery to everyone—regulations that make any kind of dialogue, or even simple brotherhood, impossible.

During the sudden total stoppage of work in France in May there was a kind of silent meditation, an interrogation of what had to be done from now on in this modern world. This understandably confused meditation could take place only because ordinary men, and particularly young people, came to the decision that their leaders had failed them.

THE EXPLOSION OF MAY

Everywhere a real debate took place—between students and professors in the universities, between wage-earners and managers in the factories—the simple and sometimes violent dispute quickly turned into a natural demand for responsibility.

Confronted with this new situation in practically all industrial societies, we can envisage one of two reactions—conservative withdrawal or forward movement. There are clear risks on both sides.

5

Between Withdrawal
and Movement

Withdrawal would mean that we prefer to put a new coat of paint on the old system of "security, irresponsibility, and stagnation." It would be to allow a revival of protectionism, which would become the unavoidable result of demagogic concessions, and of authoritarian absolutism, which would be made unavoidable by widespread disorder. Those who took part in the insurrection would be doubly duped if we followed such a path. The material advantages they might obtain would be ephemeral, since inflation would reduce them to nothing, and the power relationships they tried to change would remain intact.

Such a withdrawal—which is what, in France, the Gaullists ultimately stand for even though they may not realize it—would lead to a drop in the economic growth rate and mounting insecurity.

Forward movement, on the other hand, would mean two things:

1. France would unconditionally accept the industrial *competition* resulting from the opening of its frontiers to the Common Market and would double its efforts to take on all the challenges posed by this new world of free competition.

Unless the new generation considers this a necessity, with no cheating allowed, France will be cut off from one of the great adventures of our time. This suddenly released idealism is either headed for a terrible disillusionment or it will open a systematic use of the resources of science for the liberation of man.

Some intellectuals influential among youth denounce not only the abuse of the power of wealth, but economic development itself. To listen to them, development would change the French into frivolous consumers. If it is true that the privileged classes should restrain their appetites in order to allow the impoverished to reach a more decent standard of living, it is not those millions of French people earning less than $200 a month who should be sanctimoniously instructed in the virtues of thrift. Unless we want the new society we are calling for to be simply a pacifier to console the poor in their impotence, we have to begin by raising the lowest incomes (not just nominally), increasing the opportunities for secondary education for children of peasants and workers, and industrializing backward areas. All of this demands increased use of resources and more equitable distribution. Social justice, which has been so disgracefully neglected, is predicated on expansion, and expansion, by the same token, is now based on social justice.

2. France will have to be reorganized so that *responsibility* can become the axis of democracy.

This means:

Multiplying centers of initiative and decision-making.

We must "increase responsibilities at every level and place our bets on trust. In every profession there are men who would produce creatively if they were given more initiative, and if, together with greater responsibilities, they had the desire and the occasion to learn, to think, and to act." (*The American Challenge*)

BETWEEN WITHDRAWAL AND MOVEMENT

Breaking down caste and class barriers, changing human relationships within the hierarchies.

This does not mean doing away with the distinction between those who govern and those who are governed. Whoever tries to eliminate this distinction only sets up, on one side, power free from any real control and, on the other, a defenseless mass, as there was in the Soviet Union during the Stalinist period.

What is essential is that positions within the oligarchy that are obtained thanks to the accidents of birth, money, or influential relatives should no longer be held by people who are otherwise unqualified.

Within the professions we have to do away with hierarchical levels which determine a man's position in life on the basis of examinations taken when he is twenty years old. This system blocks the free circulation of men and ideas by a protectionism similar to the internal customs barriers imposed by the French monarchy before the Revolution of 1789. Consider the thousand corps which make up our civil service. These defense barriers based on examinations and statutes are chevaux-de-frise that protect each of the corps from the promotion of inferiors, encroachment of neighbors, infiltration of foreigners, and outside influence. How can people in one of these corps speak and make themselves understood in another? French society is the very image of its public administration.

Searching for a new collective consensus.

The lesson of these past wasted years is that the most difficult task is not to change ways of doing things but the way people think. If mental attitudes are not changed, then new techniques, as we have seen, are rejected or badly utilized. We cannot push through automation against the will of the workers, modernize agriculture against the objection of the farmers, convert the mines against the opposition of the miners. Beyond the political divisions natural in a reconstituted democracy there must be a far broader base of consent for public officials.

The price for having neglected these demands of modern industrial society was the loss of 5.4 per cent growth in French national income in 1968—nearly $6 billion on which the government had counted.

The obvious lesson to be drawn from this is that economic competition and the responsibility of citizens are not antagonistic, but perfectly compatible. The nation cannot be competitive if its citizens are not responsible.

An industrialized nation is far too complex to be governed efficiently by leaders who reign in solitary splendor. The most modern private firms practice group management and systematic delegation of responsibility. This is how they gain the flexibility they need for growth and creativity. Innovation is a complex process, but it cannot be imposed from the top. It begins with exchanges and contacts between groups which can communicate with one another on every level of the hierarchy. It depends upon a "system of dialogue."

If the French can soon be made aware that the real choice is between a withdrawal that cuts them off from their fundamental objectives of growth and a forward movement that will give them a chance of attaining these goals, we have little doubt what their answer will be.

6

Development
and Democracy

The Gaullist party is incapable of leading the way ahead. It is too identified with authoritarianism and has never really believed that the French are able to think for themselves or change their ways.

Its official opponent, the ossified French Left, is so firmly rooted in the old system that it is not capable of governing with any credibility.

We are now in one of those rare moments when the mentality of an entire people is going through tremendous change. It is up to the new generation to direct this movement toward real issues and not toward dead ends.

Two urgent tasks confront us: saving France from the disaster of underdevelopment and achieving a true democracy, which the great majority of Frenchmen have never known.

Both tasks are directed toward the same end —to give us control of our own destiny and put our country, and then Europe, in a position from which it can finally open itself to the second industrial revolution.

If the government, regardless of which party is in control, should from sheer cowardice accept a new round of inflation and a deterioration in our balance of payments, we could be sucked into a spiral that might well lead to civil disorder.

If France were obliged to leave the Common Market, she would lose important outlets for her surplus farm products and would again have to

sell them at the world market price. The resulting drain on the Treasury would inevitably force
lower farm prices and a drop in income for farmers.

The long-term effects would be even worse.
The efforts of French firms to win a secure place
in European or world markets would be shat-
tered for a long time to come. Having withdrawn
from international competition, there would no
longer be any incentive for modernization. Even
the present growth rate, which most people consider an inadequate base for future prosperity,
could not be maintained.

If we are going to undertake serious competition, setting our technology against the great
challenge of American industry, we will have to
go a good deal further and do a great deal more
than a government paralyzed by nationalistic
obsessions has ever dreamed.

France and her neighbors are not going to become competitive simply by knocking down

their tariff barriers. A European development strategy is essential. This involves the creation of multinational European firms, the pooling of each nation's scientific and technological research, and a common front in negotiations with the outside world.

Resurrecting the vision of a united Europe in this way could have a powerful impact on French politics. Cooperation among European universities, with the free movement of students and professors, could hasten the change in attitudes. So could the creation of European-scale businesses with multinational governing boards. Instead of the old-style executive playing the role of an absolute monarch, we could have a real team putting the delegation of power into practice. This, indeed, would be made necessary by the size of the corporations and the fact that their plants would be spread over a wide area.

A federated Europe must be more than a mere footnote in party platforms. While students all over the Continent are protesting against the old order, Europe is becoming the natural scene of the new Renaissance.

As France takes on this task of working out a new social order, organization, and efficiency, we must not commit the old mistake of treating the French as though they were incompetent. The worst kind of distortion would be to view participation as a way of buying off disorder.

What the French want is not a batch of limited, localized concessions but a coherent plan for decolonizing the country that will allow them to deal directly with the new and pressing problems of today's world.

If some of them prefer to ignore that there are restraints involved in economic competition, it is because no one has really made them understand that their own fate is at stake, not just abstract entities such as the government, the economy, or the Treasury.

If tomorrow they find themselves faced with

new responsibilities, we have to hope that they will show their wisdom and courage by refusing to choose a government that would be little more than a general assembly of interest groups.

From this point of view there would be no question, as we have said, of weakening the State, but rather of reinforcing it.

Redistribution of power is an ambiguous phrase. It might lead some to believe that the popular will is to tear the State to shreds, strip it of its power, and pillage it. On the contrary, a strong executive and a central government capable of defining national goals, of working out and putting into practice the strategies for attaining them, has never been more essential—in this nation as in other industrial societies.

Yet if it is to carry out its role, the State must stop trying to do everything by itself. It has to learn to get others to do things. It has to delegate some of the tedious tasks and give up trying to manage all the affairs of its citizens.

7

Business and
the University

Within the modern industrial firm we have to be honest enough to admit that "democratization" will be wishful thinking so long as there is no employee power—organized and equipped to be a partner rather than an obstacle—to balance the power of management.

The workers at the base tell the executives, as well as their own union hierarchy, that they are no longer satisfied to send delegates to meetings where they elect other delegates to present their grievances to the President or to the employers' association. They want to participate in the action. The base is where we have to build, for no real change in social relationships can ever come from agreements discussed and contracted at the summit.

Naturally, it is desirable that there be national agreements on the subjects for discussion, the objectives to be reached, and the limits not to be exceeded—based upon available resources. Unlike the present system, the substance of the changes have to be worked out within the firm, for that is where the workers must become citizens of an economic democracy, not simply subjects.

So far things have gone along as though there were nothing to negotiate at the corporation level. Yet that is precisely where the workers' situation has to be hammered out—determination of real wages, production norms, work rules, methods of conversion to other kinds of production when necessary, and arrangements for professional training. The creation of an employee power possessing the ability to negotiate and sign contracts obviously involves an acceptance of the role of the trade union within the corporation. This is more than symbolic, since it includes such complex guarantees as the legal protection of union leaders, payment for the time they devote to union activities, freedom to collect dues and distribute union literature in the plant, and last, though far from least, the ability of the unions to call on outside experts to examine the way the firm is being managed.

This is simply a point of departure. In the next stage it will be necessary to challenge the hereditary industrial monarchy which allows the same dynasties to reign from one generation to the next.

To determine in advance all the methods for moving beyond traditional "capitalism" would be to repeat the error of squeezing everything into a rigid mold rather than allowing the dynamic play of forces that would arise from real contractual relationships between teams speaking for management and those representing the workers.

Likewise, the universities are not going to be revitalized by the Minister of Education, even though he may be capable, but only if major decisions are made on the spot by those who come into contact with real situations every day.

These people—not the Ministry of Education —must be able to control the resources put at their disposal. They have to be given latitude to work out new programs, organize their departments, recruit their professors, choose their representatives, and determine criteria for promotion.

Those in positions of responsibility, including professors and students, will have to work out different kinds of solutions, depending on the conditions in the cities in which they live. We can reasonably hope that this diversity will produce more inventiveness than could come from uniformity, and that decisions made at the local level will be a good deal wiser than those made in government bureaus.

8

The Act of Confidence

The dynamism of our industrial economy depends upon the battle for intelligence. In order to win that battle we need individuals who realize that their future rests on what they are able to create and not on bureaucracies that scarcely understand what the stakes are.

In a world of scarcity, the military model served politics and administration as well. Any originality on the local level was considered a defeat. A highly centralized government set itself up as the perfect model. Today our situation is just the reverse. As social, economic, and technological problems become more complicated, the framework for resolving them becomes more diversified.

Obviously world hunger is a global problem, just as defense is a continental one. It is also true that many problems involving the environment of social life, urban and rural planning, and professional training must be worked out within the town, the city, or the region.

If democracy is to become a vital force, it has to work on a small scale. Yet when the French government carefully parceled out a few local freedoms in the decree of 1884, they were later taken away by financial centralization. Municipal elections do not produce a team that can run communal affairs. They simply indicate the electorate's preference for one political party or the other and provide a way of appointing canvassers to obtain decisions—either from the government-appointed *prefet* or from Paris—for which no one is fully responsible.

As a response to the widespread desire for greater responsibility and efficiency, the Club Jean Moulin has recently proposed a number of reforms: expanding the communes to a size that would permit effective management, enlarging their freedom of action and their financial resources, and electing mayors by universal suffrage. Another needed reform is the creation of urban complexes and regions free from the weight of administrative and financial tutelage.

Skepticism about man, his ability to reason and find solutions to the problems he faces in the firm, the city, the university, and the nation, turned out in May to be the Achilles heel of Gaullism.

This weakness, it is true, was shared by earlier governments and the whole business-bureaucratic-political elite of France whose disdain put such a damper on initiative and enthusiasm. Confusion, secrets, lies—these are the all-too-familiar characteristics of our leadership. Probably the first criterion by which we will be able to judge in the future whether things will really change, whether the *fundamental act of confidence* will one day be made, is whether our government-controlled television becomes free of the dogmatism and secretiveness of the bureaucracy.

This act of confidence would show that France is not so far gone that she has to live in the shadow of a father figure.

9

Without Hate or Fear

In his May 30 address to the nation about the nature of the revolt, President de Gaulle spoke of "hatred." It was the most inaccurate word he could have used, for there was none. This great movement was born and has flourished in a spirit of freedom and tolerance. Its ambition is to enlighten, not to destroy.

It is a movement that has been free from hate because it is a renaissance rather than a revolution and, like youth itself, sure of its strength.

With the blood of its young people flowing in its veins, France now faces the problem of awakening to the modern world. It is not only the President who was, and is, challenged, but everything he stands for as well—a centralized social order, an almost biological inability to adapt to movement and change.

This is why it is a waste of time to emphasize the disorderly and sometimes incoherent aspects of the revolutionary movement, or the offensively harsh language of the government.

There are always those who want to preserve things as they are and those who have nothing to lose. But this time there was a new element that left its imprint. No private property, no material possessions can assure power or even existence for individuals or for nations. In France, as in all other industrialized countries, the power of creation, intellectual capacity, invention, and innovation are now becoming the only sources of progress, wealth, and development.

WITHOUT HATE OR FEAR

The essential thing worth preserving is the knowledge and talent of individual men. This can change the relationship of competing political forces. When a man knows that his and his family's destiny, his chances of realizing his own potential, depend not on his identification with a given social order but essentially on his own worth—whatever his government's attitude toward property and whatever the corporate structure of industry—he need no longer feel alienated.

In the society we are trying to build, a worker's basic security will lie in education and continuous job training, which will guarantee not only adequate wages but also work that is useful to the community.

Are we afraid of powerful trade unions, of giving authority to those who have shown their abilities rather than to those who owe their jobs to heredity or to money? We shouldn't be, for we already know the benefits this movement could bring us once the initial, unavoidable shock waves of change have passed.

We seem to have the impression that by shaking ourselves loose from the ancestral order and respect for established institutions we will be plunged into some terrible adventure which will threaten not only our physical security but our intellectual integrity, that we ought to fight against it as though it were going to destroy us.

The opposite is true. We know very well that the impression of cohesion assumed by the established order only concealed the waning of our creative abilities and was really a historical abdication on our part. Our only hope is a kind of great leap forward—something that our parents were not able to do in the period between the Popular Front of 1936 and the outbreak of war in 1940. Such a leap—whatever occasion and form it takes—ought to be accepted with enthusiasm.

The men of this generation, who are now assuming positions of responsibility, have dissociated the idea of power or the goal of happiness from the notion of ownership of material goods. We are not afraid of modernizing the social contract.

We intend to nourish this new idealism against the dead weight of outdated traditions and institutions. We shall defend it against those, often respectable people, who want to preserve the past forever.

Let us go a step further. What the veterans' groups wanted to "put right" with their speeches and demonstrations and flags at the Arch of Triumph was a gesture—a scandalous one, to be sure—by the students who a week earlier spat on the famous Tomb of the Unknown Soldier. Symbol against symbol, this brings us to the heart of the matter.

It is obvious that the students did not spit on this unfortunate soldier who, in his anonymity, so perfectly represents all of those like himself who died in these barbaric patriotic wars. What they were really attacking—and quite rightly —was the stupidity of our perpetual system of national sovereignty raised to a supreme value. A system of sovereignties which bears war and hatred within it, just as clouds bear storms and mothers bear children.

In the name of life and freedom the students called a halt to absolute respect for death by command. This was perhaps the first serious homage ever rendered to the Unknown Soldier.

Those of us who have experienced *three* wars, each more absurd and brutal than the other, in less than twenty years, have the right to join the students in saying this.°

And those who have heard this nation's highest officials declare that our nuclear *force de frappe* (the ultimate expression of Gaullist soci-

---

° Of the twelve fighter pilots in my detachment in the Free French Forces, formed in 1943, seven were killed in Germany, Indochina, and Algeria.

ety and politics) was perhaps worthless against the Soviet Union, but could be "quite useful in case of another war with Germany," have not only the right, but also the duty, to do everything in their power so that the tidal wave that began to abolish the traditional order of things in May 1968 will finally destroy it, as awakening destroys nightmares.

10

From Spain to Sweden

The root of the problem we face in dealing with the sweeping changes of the second industrial revolution lies in the pervasive suspicion that corrupts human relationships in the nation, in business, and in the universities. A deep pessimism about society and about men (the very philosophy of the conservative parties) that induces us to devote the major part of our scientific talent to building nuclear weapons against our neighbors, a refusal to allow labor union power

[79]

into business because the executives believe that grievances must be broken down and made petty, if not actually forbidden; promulgating laws vital to the national welfare by decrees written in government offices as far removed as possible from debate, criticism, or suggestions; confining ourselves to a domestic policy of directorial authority and a foreign policy of national pretentiousness. This is what gives such power today to anything in France which instead puts the emphasis on dialogue and modesty.

Even before May it was obvious to everyone that France's domestic and foreign policies were steadily dragging her into decline. There can, of course, be no guarantee that what will eventually emerge from the debris of the old order will immediately bring more efficiency, justice, and order.

The universities, business, and the new regions are not going to be revitalized overnight as though a miracle had taken place. It will take years of hard work to do this, under the constant threat that the best-intended reforms will be corrupted by dogmatism or bureaucratic thinking.

Everything that has been won so far could be lost in a terrible wave of disillusionment. Imagination has been set loose from its chains and deserves to survive the enormous problems it faces. The task is not easy.

Yet one thing is certain: the only real gamble worth taking is forward movement, however dizzying it may seem at times, not the withdrawal that the apostles of order keep preaching. Withdrawal would merely condemn us to decadence.

What has taken place is important because of the remarkably precise diagnosis the May revolt has instinctively made of the cause of our decay: the underdevelopment of our responsibilities and freedoms.

It is no accident that the least-developed

country in industrial Europe is Spain, where the structure of society is the most rigid, and that the most developed country is Sweden, where there is equality, dialogue, and partnership. Nor is it any accident that in many measurable levels of development, France is always closer to Spain than to Sweden.

Here are three figures for comparison. In number of telephones per thousand inhabitants, Sweden has 450, Spain 95—and France 125. In number of television sets per thousand inhabitants, Sweden has 300, Spain 90—and France 150. In number of kilowatt hours of energy per person per year, Sweden produces 5500, Spain 1000—and France 2000.

Between fascist Spain and socialist Sweden, between the country where the police make the law and the country with the most powerful trade unions in the world, between the nation of the Falange and the nation of the Nobel Prize, we French find ourselves today nearer to Spain than to Sweden.

Even if the spirit of May had not grown out of such statistics, the conditions they reveal make it essential that we adopt this spirit, and not try to water it down.

Our generation faces formidable tasks, of which three are particularly important: evolving a functioning democratic society in the face of the revolution in information systems; inventing a universal order that will allow us to escape from the humiliating and threatening nuclear jungle in which we are now trapped; and, most difficult of all, creating a system of economic relations that will spare the underdeveloped world the pain of recolonization (by the unavoidable devaluation of raw materials) and spur it to the point where it can generate its own industry.

Europe will never be able to summon the energies to respond to these immensely exhilarating challenges so long as it is caught in a social straitjacket, its intellectual creativity mutilated.

It has been our lot to sit on the sidelines as the modern world takes shape without us—and therefore against us. When all is said and done, war, foreign or civil, remains the axis of our society, the *raison d'être* of its institutions, the highest concept of its politics. The social order has been arranged so that our country and its people were shut off from the second Renaissance, zealously guarded against the future, which has been damned as foreign, or possibly even domestic, "subversion." This is the way it has always been. It is up to us to make sure that one day things will be different.

APPENDIX

1

The Essence of the
Challenge

The desire for self-determination, for freedom first from physical oppression, then from social restraints, is a hallmark of our civilization.*

The day this drive weakens to the point that Europeans let "somebody bigger" do their work

---

* These excerpts, from the last chapters of *The American Challenge* (published in France in October 1967, six months before the revolt of May 1968), are included to prove that there was indeed a profound link between the fundamental situation of French society and the sudden outburst of its youth.

for them, the spirit of our civilization will have broken, as did that of the Arab and Indian civilizations centuries ago. We would be tainted by the knowledge of our own failure. Without suffering from poverty, we would nevertheless soon submit to a fatalism and depression that would end in impotence and abdication.

If the Left, particularly in France, remains what it has been, the chances for social integration—the key to change—will be nil, and so will chances for Europe to raise her technological power up to the level of world competition.

If the Left can overcome its instinctive reflexes of nervousness and fear when faced with the mounting tempo of progress and can rediscover the traditional values for which it stands, it can liberate so much energy in France and throughout Europe that all the elements in the equation can be changed. Salvation can come only through such an awakening.

A country like France cannot achieve the degree of organization and efficiency it needs to play a key role in building the European community and replying to the American challenge so long as the various participants in the political, economic, and social game continue to contradict and ignore each other. So long as management persists in opposing labor, and labor refuses to cooperate with management, so long as the government denies the legitimacy of the opposition and the opposition that of the government, none of the necessary changes can take place.

A permanent state of change alters all our theoretical ideas about the art of government. Conservatism, along with antiquated ideas of "careful management," necessarily becomes bad economics. A government that does not continually try to adapt its use of men and economic structures is a poor manager, just as an engineer who gets by on what he learned as a student is a poor technician.

The "good old wisdom" of conservatives, the cardinal virtue of traditional management, no longer serves to "maintain stability"; on the contrary, it causes insecurity, crises, and suffering.

There is no shortage of everyday examples: miners made prisoners of their condemned mines, teachers overwhelmed by crowded classes, unlivable cities, impassable roads, and unworkable telephones. Results of narrow vision and slow reflexes.

Adaptation to technological progress necessarily involves changes in the condition of wage-earners, changes which are totally different from the distribution of a few symbolic shares. It demands that the schools provide everyone, not just a favored minority, the intellectual tools that will allow them to make one or several changes of job and locale during their active life; that access to culture and the means of professional promotion be vastly increased; that job instability be compensated for by a guaranteed income during periods of reclassification and re-training; that the system of housing loans be re-formed so that moving from one part of the country to another becomes easy even for the poor. It is impossible to make the economy more flexible without freeing workers from anguish and fetters of all kinds, both physical and mental, which inhibit their own development and that of industrial production as well.

Plans which affect a man's occupation, his place of residence, and his way of life—all the principal elements of his existence—will encounter passive resistance or even sabotage if they are conceived and applied without the *participation* of those involved. To be convinced, workers have to be given specific information on the reasons for the contemplated changes, shown the difficulties involved, brought into the decisions about the methods that will be applied, and consulted through their representatives about the necessary contracts. In short,

[93]

they have to be recognized, not simply manipulated.

These transformations will demand all the patience, ability, and energy of governments determined to achieve real structural reforms—reforms that affect the balance of power in society. It is no longer a question of distributing fictitious rights to workers, but of helping them forge instruments that will allow them to participate in the exercise of power. And it means reexamining the objectives of economic expansion.

There is no reason for workers to submit to wage discipline if their standard of living and, more generally, the condition of their lives, is not improved as a result. Only the appeal of the end result expressed in concrete terms—such as housing, the future of their children, cultural advantages, shorter work hours, and access to leisure facilities—can persuade them to play by the new economic rules.

The choice of "good management" for maximum growth is not primarily a technical choice. It depends, first of all, on the answer to the question "Do we or do we not have confidence in the maturity and intelligence of the majority?" Until now Europe has answered no. If it decides to say yes, this choice would have unlimited consequences and could change the face of our societies. This act of confidence would be the single source of three policies that form a unity: investing in man's intelligence, liberating his initiative, and seeking a conscious choice for our collective future.

Growing needs and technical progress have speeded up the rate of change—but there are still brakes on the initiatives that would allow huge public organizations to adapt to change. What the crisis in the hospitals and the telephone service reveals is the failure of a system based on the assumption that government employees and customers are incapable of behaving reasonably. It is enough to read the decrees that appear in the *Journal Officiel* and look at the methods of decision-making to understand that in such a system the principal of a primary school is presumed to be incapable of buying pencils, the president of the government-owned railroads of making an important investment or firing a colleague, a city government of planning its own urban renewal. The presumption of incompetence spreads in concentric circles.

The presumption of incompetence produces its own confirmation, for it does not allow those it affects the opportunity to demonstrate or acquire the expertise which they are refused *a priori*. It breeds irresponsible conduct, thus justifying the suspicion on which it is based.

What counts is the determination to liberate initiative, and show confidence in man, at every level. All who are capable of learning and acting, but cannot do so because they are not given responsibility, would bring the community an invaluable supply of skills. Although no party has yet sought such an objective, it involves a political project of great urgency, for everything else depends on it and will be affected by it.

The training, development, and exploitation of human intelligence—these are the real resources, and there are no others. The challenge of the modern world is not ruthless, as so many Europe has known in her history, but it may be more dramatic, for it embraces everything.

We can no longer sit back and wait for the Renaissance. It is not going to be evoked by patriotic rhetoric or clarion calls left over from the age of military battles. It can come only from more subtle analysis, more rigorous thought, and more precise reasoning. It will call for a special breed of politicians, businessmen, and labor leaders.

The confrontation with the modern world is

an enormous undertaking. It means utilizing the intelligence of all the qualified men our society can train and equip. Above all, it means they must fight to the full limit of their worth and their ability—which means for their own sake. This is the political problem *par excellence.*

2

Answers to *Life*

Does that crisis [*the May revolution*] *mean that the end of Charles de Gaulle and Gaullism are in sight?*

J.-J. S.-S. Yes. Probably not for the next month, but their days are numbered.

But in fact this crisis is not so much about Gaullism. It is a much wider problem than Gaullism; and wider than France itself. It is the problem of the industrial world confronted with the acceleration of the rate of change in industry, in the laboratories, in invention, and finally intellectually. At some time or other such an acceleration gets into direct conflict with the traditional structures if they are too rigid. And when that conflict occurs, it is the structures that have to give way. If the revolt has exploded in France it's because French structures were especially rigid. Gaullism has just made them even more rigid.

Will it that revolution spread to other countries?
J.-J. S.-S. Certainly it will. France, as in 1789, is only the first country to be really shaken by this revolutionary process. It will happen in Spain eventually; it will happen in Germany where the structures are becoming more rigid since the two main parties joined into one political coalition and there is no more real public dialogue on the affairs of the state.

Does that mean that all organized industrial so-
ciety will crumble?
J.-J. S.-S. No. I believe that industrial society
is in a process of deep transformation. Whether
that transformation takes place through revolt like that we have witnessed in France in
May, or rather in a more civilized way of change,
more progressive, with more rational debates,
will depend on the special structure of each
country. All nations that have a rigid social order can expect an explosion.

What mistakes has De Gaulle committed in his
years of power?
J.-J. S.-S. De Gaulle has a remarkable intuition.
He has understood many things of his time and
launched many ideas that will probably be recognized as right by future historians: the idea of
decolonization, the idea that Europe should
cease to be dependent on the United States, the

idea of participation for employees in industrial firms; all of that is rather profound. But the essence of Gaullism is monologue and what is condemned by the spirit of May is the idea that a modern society can be governed by monologue. De Gaulle is a great ambiguity. Historically his message will, in many ways, remain valuable; but his methods are outmoded. He doesn't belong to this modern age. He cannot go on with his monologue because the fundamental demand of the revolt of May is a continuing demand for dialogue and sharing of responsibility.

Who will replace De Gaulle?
J.-J. S.-S. Those people who are able to invent new ways of sharing power and, thus, a new basis for democracy.

The first demand is for more and better information on all things. Everybody wants to know as many facts as possible so that each one can make his own judgment on the decisions that concern him. So the sharing of information must be complete and democratized. In France, for instance, the government has a monopoly on the largest means of information, television, and that is one reason for the explosion. We certainly must, in the future, have a completely free television, without any censorship, and open to debates on all problems.

That of course is essential, but it is not enough. Once a citizen possesses all the information he can get, he then wants to participate in the decisions. We shall be led to rediscovering the old idea of the Roman Forum. That is what the people want now, especially the young people. They call it "direct democracy." To sit in on the forum, discuss the problems, all problems, and have a word to say on the decisions. Of course this is utopia. But all revolutions have been in search of utopia. The problem of the new democracy will be to discover how to use the new technology to enable people to participate in the main decisions concerning their own destiny in a collective society.

The alliance between students and workers, however weak it has been in May, can it become a new force in the future? Or will it disappear once the separate demands have been met?

J.-J. S.-S. The two movements are in agreement on the essential point: the redistribution of power. The students and the workers, especially the young ones, now want to have access to all the information and to have the right to speak their mind and be listened to. I feel that the elite in both movements will want to keep that unity until the day when a new democratic structure has been invented and put to work.

Why, in the crisis of May, did De Gaulle not come back from Rumania as soon as the revolt

*exploded in France? Could he have not cooled
things down by making an immediate public
speech or gesture?*

J.-J. S.-S. De Gaulle has always put his foreign
policy as the first priority. He always thought
that he was keeping France under his spell with
his crusade for national independence on all
continents.

At the same time that De Gaulle was pressing citizens in other countries to change things
in their policies, he did not realize that he had a
problem at home. While staying in Rumania
he thought his speeches to the Rumanians
were being heard in France. But France was
not listening.

If he had come back sooner I don't really think
the course of events could have been changed
much. It would have proven that he wanted
to take his place immediately in the public debate and in a dialogue. De Gaulle always thinks
that he can decide when to speak and to whom

to speak. The fundamental demand of that revolt in May is precisely against the notion that one man can decide by himself so many things concerning so many men. Everybody wants to take part in the debate. This is in opposition to De Gaulle's temperament. A man of his genius and his age will find it very difficult to change his temperament.

It was in fact the students who were responsible for the fall of Lyndon Johnson in the United States, for the fall of Novotny in Czechoslovakia, and perhaps some day for the fall of De Gaulle in France. Does that mean that old men can no longer govern nations that are growing younger in population and spirit?

J.-J. S.-S. I believe this is true. But not really because of the physical age of these men, more because of their mental structures. The people who were born into the world of nuclear weapons and the world of computers have a completely different mental attitude. The problem for leaders is to have an open mind on this complicated new world, on all these sophisticated new questions, and to search for new answers. The traditional answers are not accepted any more and are not acceptable.

What mistakes has the government made in the handling of the May crisis?

J.-J. S.-S. The main one was to send the police against the students. It was that act that transformed the movement into a revolt that could not be controlled any more and became a political crisis. Without the police we would probably have witnessed a more progressive evolution. Not a revolt. In time it would have come to the same point, to the same demands, to the same necessary mutations; as it will in Spain, in Germany, in Italy, and in all industrial societies.

Has not De Gaulle spent too much money to build his nuclear deterrent and not enough to transform the social structures of France?

J.-J. S.-S. No, it is not a question of money. Questions of money, I believe, are not essential questions in the industrial world any more. It is a question of political priority and, so to speak, of psychological priority. The fact that De Gaulle has given highest priority to a nuclear deterrent is an intellectual error. French citizens want to put the highest priority on the development of French society; not on the nuclear deterrent, which is a myth.

How will the French Communist Party come out of the crisis—strengthened or weakened?

J.-J. S.-S. The French Communist Party is traumatized by the crisis like all the other centers of power in our society. The Communists will enter into a process of great change, hopefully positive change, since they not only have to consider the events in France but the events in Czechoslovakia.

All the Communist parties in Europe are re-

defining themselves, their identity, by reference
to Czechoslovakia. They will have to think
how is it conceivable to build socialism without
what they call "the dictatorship of the proletar-
iat." French society, for one, will not accept
such dictatorship, will not accept socialism without freedom. The questions that were defined in
Prague might some day find their answers in
Paris.

*Has the French revolt been provoked in some
way by the jealousy of the students or the workers against the way of life and the comfort of
American students and American workers?*
J.-J. S.-S. I don't think so. Neither has it been
emulating the Russian model. Communists
in Western Europe are trying to think through
all the questions anew because they consider
Soviet society bureaucratic and inefficient. The
students and the workers are not jealous of the
American way of life. They think America is

a dynamic society, but often cruel and unjust. So they want to invent a new society that will certainly not be modeled on the pattern of the Soviets but that will also be different from the American model. There lies the challenge. It is both a political demand and a moral demand; France and Western Europe have to find their own way.

Is it conceivable that France could fall into chaos?
J.-J. S.-S. Yes, it is conceivable.

The perspective of such possible chaos—isn't that very disturbing to you?
J.-J. S.-S. Yes, of course. But I am also disturbed by the rigidity and stagnation of France and Europe: their lack of response to the American challenge. I am rather encouraged by the mood of the revolt. From now on citizens in all sectors of industrial life will certainly take a greater

part in the process of change. So that one can hope that instead of sliding slowly into disorder we shall find a new kind of order; we shall construct a new "social contract," since the traditional one is not respected any more.

How do you feel personally toward that new generation of students revolting against their university and their government?

J.-J. S.-S. I feel that their passion is of their age and that I am not a young student myself any more. Those in their twenties have to ask the questions with the greatest possible passion and that is what they are doing. Those in their forties have another problem, that of trying to find some answers. A more sober task.

[Answers to questions by *Life* magazine in Paris, May 1968]

J.-J. Servan-Schreiber is the founder and publisher of two French publications, *l'Express*, the newsmagazine, and *l'Expansion*, a business magazine.

Born in 1924, he fled from his country in 1943 and joined the Free French Forces as a U.S.-trained fighter pilot. After the war he finished his studies as an engineer at the Ecole Polytechnique, and then became a foreign affairs correspondent for *Le Monde*. During 1956 and 1957 he served in the Algerian War, later writing a book about his experiences entitled *Lieutenant in Algeria*. The book resulted in the author's indictment by the Minister of National Defense for "weakening the morale of the French Army." However, M. Servan-Schreiber was acquitted in the trial which ensued. In 1967 he published the international best-seller *The American Challenge*. He is a close associate of two French leaders of the liberal Left: Pierre Mendès-France and Gaston Defferre.